20th Century
PERSPECTIVES

The Russian Revolution

Tony Allan

Heinemann
LIBRARY

 www.heinemann.co.uk
Visit our website to find out more information about Heinemann Library books.

To order:
 Phone 44 (0) 1865 888066
Send a fax to 44 (0) 1865 314091
 Visit the Heinemann Bookshop at www.heinemann.co.uk to browse our catalogue
and order online.

First published in Great Britain by Heinemann Library,
Halley Court, Jordan Hill, Oxford OX2 8EJ,
a division of Reed Educational and Professional Publishing Ltd.
Heinemann is a registered trademark of Reed Educational and Professional Publishing Ltd.

OXFORD MELBOURNE AUCKLAND
JOHANNESBURG BLANTYRE GABORONE
IBADAN PORTSMOUTH (NH) USA CHICAGO

Produced for Heinemann Library by Discovery Books Ltd
Designed by Ian Winton
Consultant: Martyn Rady of the School of Slavonic & East European Studies
Originated by Dot Gradations
Printed by Wing King Tong in Hong Kong, China

ISBN 0 431 12004 8
06 05 04 03 02
10 9 8 7 6 5 4 3 2 1

British Library Cataloguing in Publication Data
Allan, Tony, 1946 –
  The Russian Revolution. – (20th century perspectives)
  1.Russia – History – February Revolution, 1917 – Juvenile literature
  2.Soviet Union – History – Revolution, 1917-1921 – Juvenile literature
  I.Title
  947' .0841

Acknowledgements
The publishers would like to thank the following for permission to reproduce photographs:
Mary Evans, pp. 5, 13; Hulton Getty, p 40; Popperfoto, pp. 41, 42, 43. All other pictures reproduced
with permission of David King Collection.

Cover photograph reproduced with permission of David King Collection

Every effort has been made to contact copyright holders of any material reproduced in this book.
Any omissions will be rectified in subsequent printings if notice is given to the publishers.

Any words appearing in the text in bold, **like this**, are explained in the glossary.

Contents

What was the Russian Revolution?

The evening of 7 November 1917, was a bitterly cold one in Petrograd (modern St Petersburg). The troops who hurried through the streets of the Russian capital had their greatcoats buttoned up against the winter chill. Everyone knew that something was up. The **Bolsheviks**, a small, **left-wing** political party that had recently won the support of many of the capital's hundreds of thousands of discontented workers and soldiers, had called for revolution. Even so, theatres and restaurants were open as normal, though the night-time calm was sometimes broken by the rumble of distant guns.

By midnight, the Winter Palace was the centre of attention. It was here that the **tsar**, Russia's powerful ruler, had lived when he was in his capital city. Now, the nation no longer had a tsar. Instead, the palace housed representatives of the **Provisional Government**, set up eight months earlier to rule the country in his place. Many of the troops guarding the palace had thrown in their lot with the Bolshevik revolutionaries, and so only a few hundred soldiers remained behind to protect it. They were no match for the Bolsheviks' well-armed **Red Guards**, and when the revolutionaries finally came, shortly after midnight, the troops guarding the palace gave in almost without a fight. Within a couple of hours, the Bolsheviks — who just months before had represented only a tiny minority of the country — had taken control of the capital city.

*A dramatic **propaganda** painting shows Bolshevik soldiers and workers preparing to storm the Winter Palace in St Petersburg. In fact the building was almost undefended.*

The year of two revolutions

The fall of the Winter Palace was the final act in an amazing drama. During 1917, Russia had experienced two separate revolutions. At the start of the year, power still lay in the hands of the tsar, as it had done for the past 350 years. For almost a century, though, opposition to these all-powerful rulers had been growing, as new ideas of **democracy** and progress spread across Europe. Matters had come to a head in March 1917 when the Russian people, exhausted after three disastrous years of fighting against Germany and **Austria-Hungary** in World War One had risen up and overthrown the last of their tsars, Nicholas II. Russia had seemed to be on the verge of democracy at last.

In fact, things had gone wrong from the start. The Provisional Government, uniting all the nation's democratic forces, had struggled to maintain control in the face of mounting chaos, just as the tsar had done earlier. One political party had stood outside this Provisional Government, pouring scorn on their efforts. This was the Bolshevik Party, who called instead for all-out revolution under the slogan of 'Peace, Land and Bread'. As things went from bad to worse in the war and hunger spread across the land, the Bolsheviks' simple message had won growing support. At last, on 7 November, they struck. After just eight months, democracy had failed. Russia had moved from one kind of **dictatorship** to another; from the uncontrolled power of the tsar to the unelected leaders of the Bolshevik Party.

Tsar Nicholas II in 1894 at the beginning of his reign. The last tsar of Russia had little understanding of the changes that were taking place in his country. He was blamed for Russian defeats in World War One and was forced to abdicate in March 1917.

Revolution

Revolution is the violent overthrow of a system of government and its replacement by another. The first such major upheaval in modern times was the French Revolution of 1789, which led to the collapse of the monarchy and the execution of King Louis XVI. More recent examples include the **communist** take-over of China in 1949 and Fidel Castro's seizure of power in Cuba ten years later. The word revolution can also be used to describe other great changes in history such as the Industrial Revolution, which introduced the use of machines to produce goods that previously had been made by hand.

Russia under the tsars

The land of the **tsars** was vast. Stretching 8000 kilometres (5000 miles) from the German border to the Pacific Ocean, it covered one-sixth of the world's land area and spread across the two continents of Europe and Asia. Russians themselves made up less than half of its rapidly growing population, which had reached 130 million by the year 1900. There were also Finns, Poles, Ukrainians, Armenians, Jews, Mongols and dozens of others, speaking many different languages and dialects, all linked only by the tsar's rule.

A land of peasants

While the Industrial Revolution had brought new wealth to rival nations like Britain and Germany, Russia remained mostly a land of peasants. They made up four-fifths of the population. Some people alive in 1917 could still remember a time when the peasants had been **serfs**, bound to serve the owner of the land on which they were born. Serfdom had finally been ended by Tsar Alexander II, in 1861. Although there had been great hopes for a new Russia at the time, the life of the people had hardly changed at all. In years of bad harvests famine and starvation were common, carrying off the old, the young and the sick.

Even so, Russia as a whole had not stood still. Under a capable minister of finance, Count Sergei Witte, the country had started to **industrialize**. The Trans-Siberian Railway, the most ambitious engineering project of its day, had been built, making it possible to travel all the way from Moscow to the Pacific Ocean. In half a dozen different centres, mostly in European Russia, heavy industry gained a foothold. In the 1890s the Russian economy as a whole grew at a rate of eight per cent, the highest in Europe.

The Russian Empire in 1900.

The plight of the poor

Yet many fundamental problems remained. To begin with, the new wealth was not evenly spread. Even in the cities where the new industries were based, the workers who manned the factories lived in wretched poverty. A survey in 1904 revealed that those workers who had homes were living on average six to a room, while others slept on planks of wood beside their machines at the factories where they worked. The countryside, where most of the population lived, saw little benefit from the new money. If anything, the peasants were worse off, because taxes had to be raised to help pay for the new factories and railways. The education system remained primitive. In 1897 only one in five of the population could read or write. The sheer size of the country was itself a problem with many borders to defend and different peoples to rule. The tsar's administration — provincial governors, police, soldiers — was stretched thin.

Yoked together in a chain, women haul a barge along the River Volga in 1913. In many parts of Russia, peasants – male or female – were treated little better than animals.

It would have taken an exceptional ruler to successfully govern this vast, under-developed land. Unfortunately, Nicholas II, who came to the throne at the age of 26 on his father's death in 1894, was not up to the job. A devoted family man, he had little interest in, or talent for, ruling. Yet he clung to the notion that it was his duty not to share power. This stubborn attitude would eventually lead to his downfall.

Nicholas the autocrat

Despite his famous charm, Tsar Nicholas II had no sympathy for reform, and thought that his duty was to pass on to his son all the royal powers he himself had inherited. On coming to the throne, he announced: *'Everyone should know that in devoting all my strength on behalf of the welfare of my people, I shall defend the principle of* **autocracy** *as unswervingly as my dead father.'*

The revolutionaries

The **tsar's** view that the people should have no say in governing Russia was challenged. Ever since the French Revolution of 1789 had spread ideas of **democracy** and **human rights** around Europe, there had been voices raised to demand greater political freedom. Such talk in Russia was dangerous. Anyone questioning the tsar's power was treated as a traitor and was liable to arrest and imprisonment, or else to **exile** in the remote frozen wastes of Siberia in eastern Russia.

Terror and counter-terror

Without any legal means of discussing their grievances, some people turned to secret plotting. The first such group, the Decembrists (an anti-tsarist group), sought only to put limits on the power of the ruler. But when five of their leaders were executed in 1825 for their actions, further generations of **radicals** turned to more extreme measures. In response the tsars' ministers created a powerful secret police force to hunt down the revolutionaries, and a deadly cat-and-mouse game of terror and counter-terror began. Things came to a head in 1881, when a group called the 'People's Will' succeeded in **assassinating** Alexander II, the reforming tsar who had freed the **serfs**.

*Russian society as seen in a pre-1914 political cartoon. The tsar and the **aristocracy** at the top are supported by the Church, the army and the wealthy middle classes – all resting on the shoulders of the long-suffering workers and peasants.*

Those responsible for Alexander's murder were hunted down and executed, but other groups sprang up in their place. By the start of the 20th century they were grouped into two main factions. One, the **Social Revolutionaries**, had deep roots in the Russian countryside, and sought to stir the peasants, who made up the bulk of the nation's population, to revolt. Some sought to achieve this goal peacefully, through **propaganda** and persuasion, but there was also an armed wing of the movement dedicated to terror and political assassination. Over the next twenty years the list of their victims lengthened: it included one prime minister and three other senior ministers, an uncle of the tsar, the governor general of Finland, and several high ranking police officials. One casualty was V. K. Plehve, who as a much-feared minister of the interior had been the tsar's right-hand man and the radicals' fiercest opponent.

Karl Marx

Karl Marx (1818–83) was a German philosopher who spent much of his life in exile. He believed that the struggle between different social classes was the driving force behind history, and that ultimately power would end up in the hands of the working class because they were responsible for creating the wealth of nations. His ideas were hugely influential, helping to inspire **communism**, the political movement dedicated to creating a more equal society in which private property is abolished.

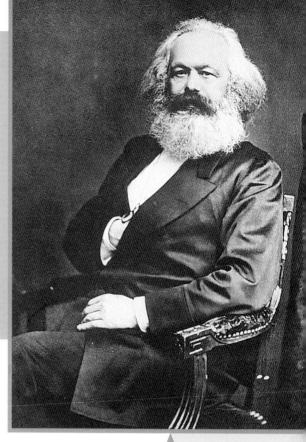

Bolsheviks and Mensheviks

The other main wing of the revolutionary movement were the **Social Democrats**, who drew their strength from the cities. They shared the views of the German political philosopher Karl Marx, who believed that the tide of history must inevitably put power in the hands of the industrial **working class**. In 1903, however, the movement split into two rival wings, divided over the tactics to adopt to bring about a working-class revolution. One group thought that the only way to achieve their goal was through a tightly disciplined party carrying out the decisions of a small, dedicated leadership group. The other wanted a more **democratic** approach, opening up the party to all who wished to join and accepting the will of the majority in decision-making. The dispute came to a head at a conference held in Brussels — for such meetings could not be held in Russia, where all political activity was banned. The first group carried the vote on the day, and from that time on bore the name of **Bolsheviks**, meaning 'the majority', while their opponents became known as the **Mensheviks**, or 'minority'. Ironically, that vote was exceptional as for most of the time up to the 1917 revolution, the Mensheviks had greater popular support.

Other groups also refused to accept the existing political situation in Russia. The Anarchists wanted to bring the state down by any means, while the liberals sought parliamentary democracy along **Western** European lines. This liberal group became known as the Constitutional Democrats, or **'Cadets'** for short. They had given up violence in favour of peaceful change, and they too were to play an important part in the 1917 revolution.

The German political philosopher Karl Marx, co-author of The Communist Manifesto, *was a guiding light for both the Bolshevik and Menshevik wings of the Social Democratic Party.*

Lenin

The man who did more than any other to transform the old Russia was born Vladimir Ulyanov at Simbirsk on the Volga River in 1870. He was 30 years old when he adopted the name Lenin, borrowed from the River Lena in Siberia. The future revolutionary was the son of well-off middle-class parents. His father had the important job of school inspector and so had to be addressed by ordinary people as 'Your Excellency'. As a boy, Vladimir enjoyed a carefree childhood growing up on the family estate until 1887, when an event happened that changed his life. His elder brother Alexander, a student who had become involved in **radical** politics, was arrested for his part in a plot to kill **Tsar** Alexander III. He had made the bomb that was to blow up the ruler and was subsequently hanged, along with four of his fellow plotters.

This oil painting shows the young Lenin comforting his mother as she grieves for her eldest son, executed in 1887 for his part in a plot to kill the tsar.

Deeply shocked, Lenin himself took up where his brother had left off. Expelled from the University of Kazan for political activities, he was eventually allowed to return to complete his training as a lawyer in 1891. He then moved to the capital St Petersburg, where he soon came to the attention of the secret police. Arrested for revolutionary activities, he spent a year in prison, and was then **exiled** to Siberia for three more years. By the time he returned to St Petersburg in 1900, he was a confirmed **Marxist**, convinced that revolution would come from the industrial **working class**. He had also developed the view that it should be led by a small group of dedicated revolutionaries — an idea that he would later champion when he became leader of the **Bolsheviks**.

Life in exile

He spent the next seventeen years up to the revolution in exile in western Europe, keeping out of reach of the tsar's police. There he wrote pamphlets, attended conferences of Russian opposition parties and edited newspapers that were smuggled into Russia. Although he devoted his life to the cause of the workers and peasants, he had little contact with them as people and could be ruthless in his attitude towards them. In 1891 he argued

against providing food aid to starving peasants on the grounds that hunger was likely to make them more radical. Having taken up the cause of revolution, he gave his entire life to it, and when the chance came in 1917 his extraordinary singlemindedness was to play a decisive part in the Bolshevik victory.

As Lenin was starting his long exile, other leading players were also taking up the revolutionary cause. In the southern region of Georgia, Josef Dzhugashvili, the son of a shoemaker, gave up training to become a priest and turned to the life of a brigand, robbing banks to raise money for **left-wing** causes. He would later rise to fame as Lenin's eventual successor, the **dictator** Josef Stalin. Another revolutionary who also changed his name was Lev Davidovitch Bronstein, who became known as Leon Trotsky. For a long while Trotsky was a **Menshevik**, but later became a close ally of Lenin in establishing the Bolshevik state. After Lenin's death, Trotsky and Stalin became bitter rivals in the race to succeed him.

Unlike the political prisoners pictured here, Lenin was not imprisoned or forced to do hard labour during his three year exile in Siberia. In fact he was able to carry on with his revolutionary writings.

Lenin the man

In *Ten Days that Shook the World*, the American journalist John Reed described the impression the Bolshevik leader made upon him in 1917: 'A short, stocky figure with a big head set down on his shoulders, bald and bulging. Little eyes, a snubbish nose, wide, generous mouth and heavy chin; clean-shaven now but beginning to bristle with the well-known beard. Dressed in shabby clothes, his trousers much too long for him. Unimpressive, to be the idol of a mob, loved and worshipped as perhaps few leaders in history have been.'

The gathering storm

In 1901, after ten years of rapid expansion, the Russian economy hit a rocky patch. In line with a general European slowdown, annual economic growth rates fell from 8 per cent to just 1.4 per cent. At the same time, a string of bad harvests brought hunger in their wake.

In the countryside discontent came to the boil. Even after the abolition of **serfdom**, it was difficult for peasants to own land. All land that was not part of the noblemen's estates was the property of the village commune, which dealt out the holdings, divided up into strips, to

Unemployed workers enjoy a meal in a soup kitchen in St Petersburg before World War One.

individual families. Most households could not make a living from the plot alone, so the sons had to spend part of each year either working for hire on noblemen's estates or else in the cities, labouring in factories. By the 1900s, there were about nine million of these travelling workers, most of them young and restless.

Meanwhile the workers in the cities were also unhappy. Wages were low and working conditions were bad. **Trade unions** were banned, so there was no way for working people to make their feelings known, except to go on **strike**, which they often did.

In response, from 1900 onwards the police authorities themselves secretly helped to set up some workers' associations. They hoped to channel the workers' anger into organizations that remained loyal to the **tsar**. Yet the strategy backfired. So many people flocked to join these associations that the government quickly grew nervous and stopped lending their support.

Life in the cities

Life for workers in the cities could be grim. One factory employee described conditions in Moscow in 1900: 'I lived near the factory, in a large, smelly house inhabited by various poor people. About fifteen of us rented one apartment. I was in a dark, windowless corner room. It was dirty and stuffy, full of bedbugs and fleas. There was just room for two wooden beds. I shared mine with one other man. The rooms stank of the mud from the streets, which was made up of dirt, rubbish and sewage.'

Even the well-off middle classes were restless for change. Doctors, lawyers and businessmen were often highly educated. They bitterly resented the fact that, because all political power remained in the hands of the tsar, they had no say in the running of the country. Some had got involved in the zemstvos — local councils first set up under the reforming

Under the gaze of an Orthodox priest, coffins of Russian soldiers killed in the Russo–Japanese War of 1904-05 are loaded onto wagons for transport to burial grounds.

Tsar Alexander II in 1864 to provide some regional welfare services such as schools and hospitals. The zemstvo activists mostly shared a taste for social reform with a belief in **Western** parliamentary **democracy**.

The Russo-Japanese war

In 1904 the growing rumble of unrest led the tsar's ministers into a fatal error. In the far east, a dispute with Japan over trading rights in Korea and northern China was escalating. Rather than settle the problem through **diplomacy**, the government decided to run the risk of entering what one minister called 'a short, victorious war' in the hope of uniting the country behind the tsar. Yet when the Japanese attacked in 1904, the country's military were taken by surprise. Russia suffered a number of humiliating defeats, all the more unexpected because the government had badly underestimated the fighting ability of their Japanese enemy.

Far from shoring up support for the tsar, the string of military disasters brought the nation's simmering discontent to the boil. The war disrupted transport, increased government expenditure and brought further food shortages. Strikes and demonstrations broke out in many parts of the country, and there were a string of terrorist **assassinations**. Defeat showed that the government was not just dictatorial but also inefficient. The angry public was ready for revolt.

Bloody Sunday

In his priest's robes, Father Gapon, the leader of the demonstration attacked by Tsarist troops on Bloody Sunday in 1905, poses alongside St Petersburg's police chief before the trouble begins.

The trigger for revolt came in January 1905 with a **strike** at St Petersburg's giant Putilov ironworks. Workers elsewhere in the city laid down their tools in sympathy, and soon much of the city's industry was at a standstill. At this moment one of the unions recently set up with secret police support came to the fore. Its leader was a priest, Father Georgi Gapon. Though fervently loyal to **Tsar** Nicholas II, he decided to lead a demonstration to the Winter Palace to present the people's grievances to the ruler. Surely, he reckoned, Nicholas would hear their complaints and take steps to correct them.

On Sunday, 22 January, Gapon set out at the head of a crowd 150,000 strong, singing hymns and carrying religious images. The demonstrators were unarmed and included many women and children. Knowing the brutal reputation of the imperial guards, however, some people

expected trouble. All too soon their fears were realized. When the marchers reached the palace, they were met by a line of **infantry** who fired two warning volleys into the air and then shot directly into the crowd, killing 40 people. The rest scattered. Throughout the day there were further bloody clashes with troops, and in all, roughly 200 people died.

As news of the 'Bloody Sunday' massacre spread across Russia, the effect on people's attitudes was dramatic. Until then, most people had believed that the tsar — the Father of the Nation — was on their side, even if his government was cruel and incompetent. Now that faith was largely gone. Father Gapon himself wrote bitterly, 'We no longer have a tsar. Today a river of blood divides him from the Russian people.'

Chaos in the countryside

Over the following months, as the war with Japan went from bad to worse, violence spread across the land. In the countryside, there was a wave of attacks on noblemen's homes, with nearly 3000 manor houses burned down, almost one-sixth of the total number across the nation. In the cities, crime rates soared and a wave of strikes paralyzed industry and the railways, making it impossible to bring the troops back from the far eastern battlefront. Russia's minority peoples saw the widespread breakdown of law and order as an opportunity to reach for freedom. In Poland there was fighting in the streets, in Finland the Russian governor general was **assassinated**, while for a time parts of Georgia broke away entirely from government control.

Disgruntled by defeat, many military units **mutinied**. The crew of one battleship, the *Potemkin*, seized control of the vessel and sailed it across the Black Sea to Romania. The wave of terrorist assassinations increased. One of the victims was the tsar's uncle, Grand Duke Sergei. Seeking scapegoats for the troubles, **right-wing** thugs launched attacks on Jewish communities, killing an estimated 3000 people.

Rise of the soviets

In Moscow and St Petersburg, the troubles came to a head in September and October with a general strike that brought industry to a standstill. To bring some sort of order to the chaos, the workers set up **soviets** — a Russian word meaning 'councils' — to keep basic services functioning. Soon these were virtually running the cities. Sensing revolution in the air, some political **exiles** slipped back into Russia. Trotsky became a leading light of the St Petersburg soviet, ending up as its chairman, but Lenin arrived late and played little part.

The fact was that the 1905 uprising had taken the revolutionaries by surprise as much as it had the government. Springing up in many different places for many different causes, it was formless and uncontrolled, and for a time at least Russia seemed to be falling apart.

*Taken in October 1905 this photograph shows workers parading through St Petersburg carrying banners calling for **democratic** reforms and an end to one-man rule.*

The October Manifesto

Russia was saved from total collapse in 1905 largely because the various uprisings were uncontrolled. Together, they might have been unstoppable, but separately each one could be put down by the **tsar's** forces.

A vital first step towards restoring order was ending the war. As it turned out, Count Witte was able to make peace with Japan on surprisingly favourable terms at the Treaty of Portsmouth, signed in September. Yet even so, the nation remained in chaos, and the general **strike** that had been called in the cities threatened to make it ungovernable. In October, Witte presented the tsar with a stark choice: either he would have to appoint a military **dictator** to restore order by force, or make concessions to his opponents, who were clamouring for **democratic** reform. At first Nicholas favoured the first idea, but when his choice of dictator, the Grand Duke Nicolai, threatened to shoot himself if Nicholas refused to bow to public opinion the tsar unwillingly agreed to sign the document that Witte had prepared.

*This anti-tsarist **propaganda** image shows the October Manifesto imprinted with a bloody hand. The hand was meant to represent the oppressive tsarist government.*

This document, which became known as the 'October Manifesto', announced that for the first time in its history Russia would have an elected parliament, the **Duma**. Political parties and **trade unions** were legalized, **censorship** was to be lifted, and some **political prisoners** were set free.

Life returns to normal

The manifesto was a limited move in the direction of reform — the parliament was only to be able to advise the tsar, not to make laws — but it was enough to split the opposition to the tsar. The liberals at once withdrew their support for the general strike, which quickly crumbled. With peace and the ending of the rail strike, troops

---

The world turned upside down

In Boris Pasternak's novel *Doctor Zhivago*, Marfa Tiverzina, an engine-driver's widow gives her son news of the October Manifesto, expressing the hopes it aroused among ordinary people for better times ahead:
'Think of it! The tsar has signed a manifesto and everything's to be turned upside down! Everybody's to be treated right, the peasants are to have land, and we're all going to be equal with the gentry!'

began to return from the far east and were quickly used to restore order. The St Petersburg **soviet** was broken up, as were those in other cities. In Moscow this led to street fighting that claimed more than 1000 lives. The violence in the countryside proved even more difficult to quell. It surged up again in 1906, and was only put down with much brutality. As many as 15,000 people are thought to have been executed.

State dignitaries gather for the official opening of the Duma, Russia's first elected parliament, in May 1906.

The October Manifesto had raised great hopes, but in the end these were quickly crushed. Censorship was reimposed and political prisoners were rearrested. Some revolutionaries, like Lenin, once again fled the country. Trotsky was seized when the St Petersburg soviet was closed down, and he was **exiled** to Siberia.

Russia's first Duma

The parliamentary democracy promised in the manifesto also fell short of expectations. With order restored in 1906, the tsar felt sure enough of his position to issue the 'Fundamental Laws', which reasserted his own unrestricted authority, stating bluntly that, 'The All-Russian Emperor possesses the supreme **autocratic** power; not only fear and conscience, but God himself, command obedience to his authority.' In keeping with this view, Nicholas treated the Duma with barely-hidden contempt. When the first Duma proved too **radical** for his liking, he simply dissolved it. A second Duma suffered a similar fate. To make the Duma more compliant he ordered a change to the electoral rules. When the third Duma was called in 1907, two-thirds of its delegates were elected by the richest one per cent of the population.

Even so, order had been restored, and a strife-weary population mostly seemed happy to get back to normal life. On the surface little had changed, but in reality the tsar's position had been seriously weakened, and he was never to exercise the same unchallenged authority again.

The coming of World War One

By agreeing to set up the **Duma**, the **tsar** had managed to split the groups opposed to his rule. Those who wanted parliamentary **democracy** similar to that in **Western** European countries — mostly the middle classes — were by and large happy for the time being to give the new body a chance. The rest — workers and peasants — were still discontented, but were not strong enough on their own to bring the system down. It seemed tsarist Russia had survived.

Stolypin's strong measures

To shore up his position further, Nicholas II now turned to an able administrator, Peter Stolypin. The son of landowning **aristocrats**, Stolypin believed in the need for strong measures to save the nation. First, he cracked down on the **left-wing** parties, closing **trade unions** and left-wing newspapers. Then he set about introducing **radical** reforms of his own in the countryside. Peasants who so wished could, for the first time, leave the village communes and own their own land. The idea was that the ablest and most ambitious peasants would develop into a class of independent small landholders who would respect property rights and be loyal to the tsar.

Stolypin's reforms attracted bitter hostility, both from traditionalist peasants, who feared the loss of commune lands, and from aristocratic landowners, who saw it as a threat to their own position. Even so, the changes were effective, at least in parts of the nation. Agricultural productivity improved dramatically with an increase of 20 per cent in the grain crop between 1908 and 1912. At the same time, Count Witte had negotiated a huge loan from western European bankers that got Russian industry moving again, increasing the rate of growth from just 1.5 per cent a year during 1900–05 to over 6 per cent between 1907 and 1914. Between 1900 and 1914 coal production more than doubled and steel output grew by over 50 per cent.

Peter Stolypin, Russia's prime minister from 1906, poses with his wife. Stolypin was assassinated at the opera house in Kiev in 1911.

The death of Stolypin

Politically, however, there was less progress. With the change in the electoral laws, the Duma became the mouthpiece of the wealthy landowners. Without any legal means of making their voices heard, the radicals turned again to violence. Even in 1908, a quiet year, some 1800 officials were killed in political attacks across Russia. Eventually Stolypin himself fell victim. In 1911 he was shot dead while attending an opera in Kiev.

Without his leadership, the tsar's government again became directionless. Some ministers tried to boost support for the ruler by stirring up hostility against Russia's Jewish population, traditional targets for **right-wing** hatred. When that proved insufficient, nationalist opinion looked for foreign enemies instead. Tensions in the Balkan region just beyond Russia's south-western border came to a head in 1914 with the **assassination** of the heir to the **Austro-Hungarian** throne. The army and much of the Duma urged the tsar to declare war on Austria-Hungary, Russia's rival for influence in the region. Briefly Nicholas held back as other advisers pointed out that Russia's last two military campaigns, in the **Crimean** and Russo-Japanese wars, had both been disastrous for the monarchy; one had stirred up the agitation that led to the **emancipation** of the **serfs**, the other to the 1905 uprising and the October Manifesto. But in the end the voices for war were loudest. On 30 July 1914 the tsar ordered a general **mobilization** of the troops, and within a week Russia was at war not just with Austria-Hungary but with Germany as well. World War One had begun.

Taken early in World War One, this photograph shows Russian officers kneeling before Nicholas II (on horseback). The tsar holds an icon (sacred painting) to confer blessings on them.

The shadow of Rasputin

For the first few weeks after the declaration of war, it seemed that the **tsar's** gamble might pay off. For the first time in his reign, the country rallied behind him. On the **Austro-Hungarian** front the fighting went well, too. Russian forces under General Brusilov captured much of the province of Galicia. A spirit of **patriotism** swept across the nation and St Petersburg was even renamed Petrograd to sound more Russian. Russia was only prepared for a short war, but when German forces further north won two crucial victories at Tannenburg and the Masurian Lakes, it became obvious that there was to be no quick victory.

Unrest in the ranks

From that time on the war went from bad to worse. While Russia's enemies managed to feed, equip and move their armies as needed, the ramshackle Russian administration cracked under the strain. Soon attacks were having to be called off because the artillery (big guns) had no

Russian soldiers taken as prisoners during the early years of World War One. Russia's involvement in this war had disastrous consequences for the tsar.

shells. Casualties quickly rose into the millions as incompetent commanders sent waves of **infantry** to attack positions defended by machine-guns. Underfed, poorly clothed and ill-armed, a mood of despair spread among the troops. Some came to see their own officers — mostly from the landowning class they had come to hate — as more their enemy than the Germans or Austrians.

Things were not much better behind the lines. The need to divert trains to carry supplies to the front clogged up the nation's transport system, with the result that deliveries of food and other essentials to the cities were held up. Soon queuing for these essentials was a regular part of daily life. In the face of repeated military defeats and growing shortages, the mood of patriotism soon faded, to be replaced by anger and bitterness.

Despair on the front line

A report from a Russian general shows how bad things were for ordinary soldiers fighting on the front line as early as 1915: 'In recent battles, one-third of the men have had no rifles. The poor devils had to wait patiently until their comrades fell before their eyes, and they could pick up their weapons. The army is drowning in its own blood.'

A hated queue

By August 1915, things were going so badly that the tsar decided to take personal command of the army. It was an unwise decision. Not only did it mean that he had to take personal responsibility for the military failures but it also left the rest of the country in the hands of his wife, Tsarina Alexandra. German by birth, she was suspected unfairly of sympathizing with the enemy. She was, however, completely opposed to **democracy**, constantly encouraging her husband to be the **autocrat** that she was convinced Russia needed.

She was hated worst of all, though, for being under the sway of the sinister Grigori Rasputin. Though only a peasant, Rasputin had a reputation as a holy man. In fact he was a heavy drinker and womanizer. Nevertheless he appeared to have real gifts as a healer, and was able to win the admiration of the royal family through his ability to relieve their son's haemophilia — a rare blood disorder that made the boy liable to uncontrolled internal bleeding after even minor knocks and scrapes. The tsarina in particular came to believe that Rasputin had been sent by God to save the tsar and Russia. As his influence on policy and government appointments grew, support for the monarchy dissolved. Finally a group of noblemen took the law into their own hands and murdered Rasputin, but by then — in December 1916 — the damage had been done. The last vestiges of respect for the tsar's rule were gone. War-weary and disillusioned, Russia was ripe for revolution.

A cartoon from 1916 shows Rasputin as a sinister, looming presence, holding the tsar and tsarina as puppets on his knees.

Rasputin's sinister powers

Prince Yusupov — the nobleman who eventually killed Rasputin — describes his first encounter with the supposed holy man: *'His hypnotic power was immense. I felt it subduing me and diffusing warmth throughout the whole of my being. I grew numb; my body seemed paralysed. I tried to speak, but my tongue would not obey me, and I seemed to be falling asleep, as if under the influence of a strong drug. Yet Rasputin's eyes shone before me like a kind of phosphorescent light...'*

1917: The first revolution

When the uprising that brought down the **tsar** finally came, it took everyone by surprise. Even agitators who had spent their life trying to bring it about were unprepared. Just a month before, Lenin had declared, 'We older men perhaps will not live to see the coming revolution'.

Mutinous troops pose in Petrograd at the start of the revolution that forced the tsar to step down from power in March 1917.

With most of the revolutionaries in prison or in **exile**, the revolution was created in the streets. It began on 8 March 1917 with a demonstration of women fed up with queuing for bread. They rallied the factory workers to their cause, and the next day **striking** workers started attacking public buildings and police stations. Troops were called out to restore order, and there were some shootings, though most of the soldiers supported the demonstrators rather than their own officers. **Mutiny** spread through the army barracks, and soon thousands of armed soldiers had joined the crowds in the street. Left undefended, most of the tsar's ministers fled or went into hiding.

Two power centres

The old government quite simply collapsed. Out of the chaos, two separate power centres emerged, both housed at first in different wings of Petrograd's Tauride Palace. One was the **Provisional Government**, set up by party leaders in the **Duma**. It was called provisional because it was seen at the time as a temporary arrangement until a proper government could be established. The other was the Petrograd **Soviet** of Workers' and Soldiers' **Deputies** — a revival of the body set up in 1905.

With chaos and crime spreading in the streets, the first job was to restore order. The Provisional Government sought to do so in the name of parliamentary **democracy**, and the Soviet agreed to lend its support as long as its own demands were met. These demands included an end to **censorship**, the release of all **political prisoners**, and the creation of people's **militias** to replace the old tsarist police. Both bodies supported free elections for a **Constituent Assembly**, to be chosen by all the people.

The tsar steps down

That left the question of what to do with the tsar. On hearing of the trouble in Petrograd, he had ordered troops to the capital city to attack the demonstrators, only to find that they refused to obey him. Without their support he was powerless. There were still some **right-wing** leaders in the Duma who wanted him to stay on as a constitutional monarch, rather like the British king — while still head of state, he would have had no political power — but the idea was quickly dropped.

Others thought he should abdicate (give up the crown) in favour of his son, but Nicholas himself ruled out that idea, knowing that the boy was too sickly to be tsar. A deputation from the Duma then approached Nicholas's brother, Grand Duke Michael. When he refused the offer on 16 March, a thousand years of rule by monarchy came abruptly to an end.

The Provisional Government was now in control, but it inherited all the problems that had brought down the tsar, plus one more: divided power between the Assembly and the Soviet. Until the new Constituent Assembly could be called — the elections were eventually arranged for November — it could not claim to be democratically elected. The Soviet, in contrast, had huge popular support in the army and the factories, but no part in government. In the joyful March days, when all the talk was of the two bodies sharing 'dual power', it seemed that contradictions could be overcome if everyone worked together. In fact, though, it was only to be a matter of weeks before strains began to show.

The Soviet of Workers' and Soldiers' Deputies meets in Petrograd's Tauride Palace in April 1917. The Soviets were political organizations made up of workers, soldiers and sailors who were more radical than the members of the Provisional Government.

The tsar's legacy

Alexander Kerensky, who served in the Provisional Government first as minister of justice and then as prime minister, summed up its situation on taking power: '[The Government] *inherited nothing from the tsar but a terrible war, an acute food shortage, a paralysed transportation system, an empty treasury, and a population in a state of furious discontent...*'

The democratic experiment

Their heads shaved for protection from lice, Moscow street children survey the toppled head of a statue of Alexander III, father of Nicholas II, following the collapse of tsarist rule.

Although people could see that difficulties lay ahead, most of Russia greeted the **tsar's** downfall with joy. In a spirit of co-operation, almost all the political parties agreed to put their differences temporarily aside to work together for **democracy**. Even though the **Provisional Government** was dominated by middle-class liberals of the Constitutional Democratic (**Cadet**) party, it could also call on the support of the main **left-wing** parties, the **Mensheviks** and **Social Revolutionaries**.

Soon, the Provisional Government set about putting through the reforms that so many people had sought for so many years. **Censorship** was abolished and there was to be absolute freedom of speech. **Trade unions** and **strikes** were legalized. All the different peoples within the

Russian empire were to have equal rights, and outlying regions like Finland and Poland (both then part of Russia) were to have a say in running their own affairs. All **political prisoners** were freed and the death sentence was abolished.

Problems that would not go away

The big problems that had confronted the tsar's government, however, were not so easy to deal with. Conditions in the cities continued to worsen, as food shortages increased. Army deserters — there were two million of them by late 1917 — joined the ranks of the unemployed, living by petty crime in the streets. As for the factory workers, their expectations had been raised by the overthrow of the tsar, and they increasingly demanded a say in running industry.

In the countryside, the peasants too were impatient for change. Tired of waiting for land reform, which the Provisional Government had postponed until the **Constituent Assembly** could be called, village communes increasingly took the law into their own hands, seizing land from its private owners. Mobs started burning manor houses again, as in 1905.

Worst of all, the war refused to go away. The country was war-weary, and the soldiers wanted above all to get back home. But the Provisional Government felt that it had a duty to the nation not to give in. Besides, its ministers were under pressure from Russia's **allies**, Britain and France, to keep on fighting.

A Bolshevik-era painting shows Lenin arriving from exile to a hero's welcome at Petrograd's Finland Station on 3 April 1917. The Germans had let him pass through their territory in the hope that he would weaken the Russian war effort.

Lenin returns from exile

In addition to its other problems, the Provisional Government faced opposition from one significant party on the left: the **Bolsheviks**. In April their leader Lenin arrived back from **exile** to a hero's welcome at Petrograd's Finland Station. He had travelled by arrangement with Russia's German enemies, who — in the hope that he would stir up trouble — had transported him from his home in Switzerland through Germany in a special sealed train. Within days of his arrival, he announced his programme: total opposition to the Provisional Government, an immediate end to the war, the arming of the workers, and the passing of all power to the **soviets**. At first even his own Bolshevik supporters were shocked. Russia had just experienced one revolution and now Lenin was calling for another. Critics called his views the ravings of a madman, but events were to prove them wrong.

Discontent in the cities

Fully stretched by the war effort, the Provisional Government could do little to improve life for city-dwellers on the home front. John Reed described life in Petrograd in 1917: *'At night the street lights were few; in private houses the electricity was turned off from six o'clock until midnight. Robberies and house-breaking increased. In apartments men took turns at all night guard duty, armed with loaded rifles... Food was becoming scarce. The daily allowance of bread fell. There were times when no bread at all was available. For milk, bread, sugar and tobacco one had to queue for long hours in the cold rain...*

Of course, life for the rich went on much the same. The theatres were going every night, including Sundays.'

The Bolshevik take-over

Russia and Europe 1914–1917

Under pressure to reunite the nation, the **Provisional Government** now made a bad mistake. In July 1917 it ordered a military advance in Galicia, an area in the north east of **Austria-Hungary**. This was quickly overwhelmed by a German counterattack, leaving the Russian army in retreat with over 200,000 casualties.

Map legend:
- Area lost under Treaty of Brest-Litovsk
- ★ Battles
- Eastern Front

FINLAND
Petrograd
Moscow
RUSSIAN EMPIRE
Baltic Sea
Tannenburg ★
★ Masurian Lakes
GERMAN EMPIRE
Brest-Litovsk
Kiev
Galicia
UKRAINE
AUSTRO-HUNGARIAN EMPIRE
ROMANIA
Black Sea
GEORGIA
Caspian Sea
BULGARIA
OTTOMAN EMPIRE

The 'July days'

The move was deeply unpopular, and by mid-July there were armed mobs out on the streets of Petrograd demanding that the government should step down. Instigated by the **Bolsheviks**, the 'July days', as the riots became known, were a rehearsal for the uprising that finally brought down the Provisional Government in November, but now they had come too soon. Without leaders to direct them, the rioters dispersed.

In the wake of the riots, the **socialist** Alexander Kerensky took over as prime minister, and at once launched an assault on the Bolsheviks, whom he blamed for the unrest. Lenin, he claimed, was a German spy, trying to stir up trouble at a time when the Russian army was fighting for its life. For a time, public opinion supported him. The Bolsheviks' headquarters was shut down by police, several of their leaders were arrested, and Lenin himself had to escape in disguise to Finland.

The mood across Russia was by now feverish. Kerensky had the job of trying to hold together a country that was increasingly divided. The spirit of co-operation that had marked the downfall of the **tsar** was largely gone.

The Kornilov affair

To restore order, Kerensky appointed a new Commander-in-Chief of the army, Lev Kornilov, and for a time toyed with the idea of summoning him to Petrograd to put down the Bolsheviks once and for all. But fearing that the general intended to seize power for himself, he gave orders instead for his dismissal. Kornilov refused to step down. Instead, he determined to advance on Petrograd without Kerensky's permission.

Fearing a **right-wing** take-over, Kerensky now looked to the **left-wing** for support, and gave orders that the workers should be armed. Kornilov, meanwhile, had found that his own troops were unwilling to obey him. His last hopes of advancing on the capital faded when **striking** railwaymen prevented him from transporting his forces.

Pro-democracy demonstrators gather in Petrograd for a mass rally in 1917.

The Kornilov affair finished off Kerensky's chances of holding a middle line. Without army support, he had no troops of his own to set against the Bolshevik **Red Guard**, who had commandeered most of the rifles and machine-guns handed out from the arsenals (weapon stores) to combat Kornilov. Fearing that the revolution was in danger from the generals, workers now flocked to join the Bolsheviks, whose slogans of 'Peace, Land and Bread' and 'All Power to the **Soviets**' increasingly matched with the popular mood.

Now Lenin saw his chance. Against the wishes of most Bolsheviks, he argued that the party must strike at once, saying 'History will not forgive us if we do not take power now'. Finally his appeals won the day. Trotsky organized a military uprising. On 6 November 1917, Red Guards occupied key points across Petrograd, and on the following day, with the fall of the Winter Palace, the Provisional Government itself fell into their hands. Kerensky fled the city. Stunned, the people of Russia learned that there had been another revolution. The Bolsheviks were now in charge.

Proclaiming the revolution

On the day the Bolsheviks launched their bid for power, Lenin released this declaration:
'TO THE CITIZENS OF RUSSIA!
The Provisional Government has been deposed...
*The cause for which the people have been struggling — the immediate offer of a **democratic** peace, the abolition of landlord property rights over the land, worker control over production, the creation of a Soviet Government — this cause has been achieved.*
Long live the revolution of Workers, Soldiers and Peasants!'

Building socialism

Even the **Bolsheviks** themselves were surprised with the ease with which they had seized power, and they quickly took steps to make sure they would keep it. To the surprise of many of his own followers, Lenin refused to co-operate with the **Mensheviks** and most of the other **socialist** parties. Instead he set up a Council of People's **Commissars** that was dominated by Bolsheviks. Meanwhile, going back on earlier promises of freedom of speech, he outlawed the **Cadets** — the main **right-wing** opposition party — and closed down newspapers supporting other political groups.

Even Lenin, however, could not stop the **Constituent Assembly** from meeting. For half a century, the idea of a freely-elected parliament had been the hope of those seeking a more **democratic** Russia; and the elections had been called for shortly after the Bolsheviks seized power. Yet when the results came in, they were not at all to Lenin's liking. The Bolshevik Party had won only 24 per cent of the vote, giving it 170 seats out of a total of 707. Its vote was dwarfed by that of the **Social Revolutionary** Party which, thanks to its backing among the peasants, had won 370 seats.

Over-ruling democracy

Lenin, however, had no intention of giving up power, instead, he chose to overrule democracy. He sent troops to prevent the Assembly from meeting and his partner in power Trotsky instructed the delegates to go home, telling them, 'Your role is finished, and you may go where you belong — on the rubbish tip of history.' Soldiers opened fire on demonstrators protesting the closing, killing at least ten people.

Meanwhile Lenin set about building socialism by decree. With extraordinary speed, the Council of People's Commissars pushed through a mind-boggling number of revolutionary measures aimed at transforming the basis of Russian society. Private ownership of land was abolished, and the peasant communes were encouraged to seize landowners' property. Banks and much of industry was **nationalized** (taken over by the state). All **aristocratic** titles were done away with and in future, everyone was to be known simply as 'citizen' or 'comrade'.

An early aim of the Bolshevik government was to educate working people, as this literacy campaign poster shows.

The old criminal courts were replaced by revolutionary tribunals in which anyone could appear as a lawyer. Men and women were declared equal in law, and divorce between married couples was to be made easy. The stock market ceased to exist. All Russia's existing debts to foreign nations and bankers were cancelled, and private inheritance of goods and property was banned. The Orthodox Church lost its privileged position and was expected to pay the state rent for its churches, and religious education was banned in schools. In the rush to get rid of the past, the old Russian calendar, which ran thirteen days behind the **Western** one, was replaced; and Moscow took over from Petrograd as the nation's capital city.

Making peace with Germany

The main reason for the move to Moscow was the looming presence of enemy troops, for Bolshevik power still faced another threat that could not be dealt with as easily as the Constituent Assembly — the German army, which was now within striking distance of Petrograd itself. Despite protests from his own supporters, Lenin decided that the survival of the

revolution required peace at any price. When terms were agreed in the Treaty of Brest-Litovsk, signed in March 1918, they were disastrous for Russia. The nation lost huge amounts of land in the Baltic region, Poland, the Ukraine and Georgia. In all the losses cost it one-third of its population and more than a quarter of its agricultural land, as well as a third of its industry and nine-tenths of its coal mines. It was a heavy price to pay for the survival of the revolution.

Lenin, wearing a long dark coat, is pictured here with other Bolshevik officials in Moscow's Red Square. To escape the German armies the Bolshevik government was moved from Petrograd to Moscow in March of 1918.

Peace at any price

Early in 1918, Lenin explained to the Petrograd **soviet** why he thought it necessary to accept the harsh German terms for making peace: '*To carry on a revolutionary war we need an army, and we do not have one. It is a question of signing terms now, or of signing the death of the Soviet government three weeks later.*'

The fate of the Romanovs

Meanwhile, the **Bolsheviks'** seizure of power had not gone unchallenged inside Russia. Immediately after the November **coup**, the deposed prime minister, Alexander Kerensky, had tried to rally support in the army. Only a few troops backed him, however, and they were defeated by **Red Guards** outside Petrograd. Kerensky himself escaped into **exile**. Then, when the Bolsheviks' intention to rule alone became known, railwaymen and civil servants went on **strike** against the new government. There were even splits in the Bolshevik Party itself. At one point four of its leading members resigned in protest at Lenin's tactics, only to return to the fold shortly afterwards.

Lenin responded unrelentingly to all these challenges. The strikes were declared illegal, and the workers gradually drifted back to their jobs. A secret police organization, the **Cheka**, was set up to spy on political opponents. It would soon become even more feared than the secret police which operated under the **tsars.** Unrest in the cities was stamped out by armed Red Guards and in Moscow there was a week of street fighting that ended in a victory for the Bolsheviks.

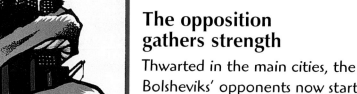

The opposition gathers strength

Thwarted in the main cities, the Bolsheviks' opponents now started grouping in outlying parts of the country. General Kornilov, along with several leading figures from the old **Provisional Government**, made his way to the Don region of southern Russia to join **Cossack** rebels there. Meanwhile, a legion of Czech soldiers who had fought on the Russian side in the war now became embroiled with Red Guards and took up arms against the Bolsheviks. Intent on fighting their way across Russia to the Pacific port of Vladivostok, they took control of the Trans-Siberian Railway, cutting the government in Petrograd off from the far-eastern provinces.

The Czechs' triumphal progress eastward was to have an unforeseen consequence that was to prove fatal for the former royal family. After the February revolution, they had at first lived at their country estate outside Petrograd, taking no part in politics and enjoying the quiet family life for which they had always been best suited. As the revolutionary temperature rose, however, the Provisional Government had transferred the tsar and his family for their own safety to Tobolsk, a rural backwater in Siberia.

In the spring of 1918, the new Bolshevik administration ordered the family to be moved again, this time to the town of Ekaterinburg near the Ural Mountains. There, on the night of 17 July 1918 with the Czech legion approaching (they captured the town a week later), the entire family were murdered, along with their doctor, their remaining servant and even their pet spaniel. At the time, the Bolshevik government blamed the killing on the local **soviet**, some of whom were subsequently put on trial. Now, however, it is known that the order had come from Moscow, and probably from Lenin himself. He was known to be concerned that **counter-revolutionaries** might use the ex-tsar as a figurehead for the opposition.

In captivity in the Siberian town of Tobolsk, the deposed Tsar Nicholas II and members of his family sit on a platform he himself had built above the greenhouse of the house where they were being held.

The night of the 17 July

Iakov Iurovskii, the leader of the firing squad that killed the royal family, describes their last moments: 'When the party entered, [I] told the Romanovs that ... the Execution Committee of the Urals Soviet had decided to shoot them. Nicholas turned his back to the detachment and faced his family. Then, as if collecting himself, he turned around, asking "What? What?" I rapidly repeated what I had said and ordered the detachment to prepare. Its members had previously been told whom to shoot and to aim directly at the heart, to avoid much blood and to be quickly done. Nicholas said no more. He turned again towards his family. The others shouted some incoherent exclamations. All this lasted a few seconds. Then the shooting began, going on for two or three minutes. I killed Nicholas on the spot.'

Civil War: Reds versus Whites

By mid 1918, the **Bolshevik** leaders were under siege. Everywhere their enemies were on the move, and for a time it seemed that the revolution itself might collapse.

Anti-Bolshevik forces — called **Whites**, to distinguish them from the **Communist** Reds — attacked on three fronts. In the south, the **Cossack** revolt had been put down, but the defeated army had regrouped under the leadership of General Denikin, who had taken control after Kornilov was killed. In the east, large parts of Siberia had declared themselves independent of the central government in Moscow. Although various factions, including **democratic socialist** groups, were originally involved, the movement finally came under the command of an ex-**tsarist** naval commander, Admiral Kolchak. In the north-west, a third army under General Yudenich grouped in Estonia to prepare an assault on Petrograd.

A visiting group of British officers liaises with White Russian forces fighting the Red Army in eastern Russia. Many foreign powers offered money and weapons to the Whites, but not much in the way of troops.

To make matters worse, Russia's wartime **allies** also decided to send troops to fight against the new government. The British and French were angry that the Bolsheviks had not just pulled out of the war with Germany without consulting them, but had also announced that they would not repay any of the huge debts that the tsar's administration had run up with **Western** bankers and governments. Both sent forces north to the White Sea ports (where American troops also landed) and south into the Black Sea. The British ended up holding the port of Archangel for more than a year, while the French seized Odessa. Meanwhile the Japanese took control of the Pacific port of Vladivostok, at the eastern end of the Trans-Siberian Railway; it was only returned to Russia in 1922.

Declaring independence

Taking advantage of the general chaos, the outlying regions of the old tsarist empire lost little time in breaking free from Russian rule. Poland had already been lost to the Germans in the course of World War One. Now Lithuania, Finland, Moldavia, the Ukraine and the three nations beyond the Caucasus Mountain range, Azerbaijan, Armenia and Georgia, all declared their independence. Once World War One had ended with a German surrender in November 1918, Poland went further, sending an army to invade Russia. In May 1920, the Poles even succeeded in capturing the Ukrainian capital of Kiev.

ГРУДЬЮ НА ЗАЩИТУ ПЕТРОГРАДА!

A **propaganda** poster urges workers and soldiers to defend Petrograd in the civil war. White forces under General Yudenich were driven back from the city in October 1919.

The Bolsheviks also had problems closer to home. The **left-wing** members of the **Social Revolutionary** party, who had agreed to enter government with them, had become increasingly unhappy with their partners. In July 1918 they **assassinated** the German ambassador to Moscow in protest against the Treaty of Brest-Litovsk, and then seized the head of the **Cheka** secret police. Their revolt, though, was more of a protest than a serious attempt to take power and was quickly put down. One month later another Social Revolutionary, a woman named Fanya Kaplan, tried to assassinate Lenin himself; shot in the neck, he was lucky to survive.

The Red Terror

The Bolsheviks' answer to the threats was the 'Red Terror'. The Cheka were given a free hand to arrest and execute all suspected enemies. They seized the chance eagerly. Anyone from a middle-class background was at risk, so too were peasants suspected of hoarding grain, or workers unhappy with the long hours they had to work to produce arms to win the war. Some of the victims were unexpected: Lenin's own cousin was executed in Siberia, while in the capital itself a clown named Bim-Bom was shot dead in front of the audience at the Moscow Circus for telling anti-Bolshevik jokes. Prisoners in Cheka jails were subjected to horrifying tortures; some of the torturers themselves are said to have gone mad as a result of what they saw. No accurate records were kept of the killings, but historians reckon that several hundred thousand people were either executed or died in Cheka prison camps — possibly more than in all the battles of the civil war.

Victory for the revolution

The threat to the **Bolsheviks** reached a climax in 1919. Early that year, Admiral Kolchak attacked from Siberia and in July Denikin's southern forces launched a three-pronged drive on Moscow. In October General Yudenich advanced on Petrograd. For a time it seemed that Kolchak and Denikin's forces might link up, putting all southern and eastern Russia in the hands of the **Whites**. Meanwhile in the far north a few British troops occupied the ports of Murmansk and Archangel. Later Britain recognized a White government in Archangel.

By mid-1920, however, all the threats had been overcome. Kolchak had been captured and executed, and his army was straggling eastward in flight towards Vladivostok. Denikin's assault had been stopped in two pitched battles in October 1919. He himself was forced to resign, and his troops retreated back to the **Crimea**, eventually to escape across the Black Sea into **exile** in British and French ships. Yudenich was defeated outside Petrograd and was driven back to Estonia, where his army broke up. Seeing the tide of battle turning, Britain, France and the other foreign powers first withdrew their own troops and then cut off the supplies of arms and money on which their White allies had largely depended.

The national uprisings were also quelled. In the north the Bolsheviks had been forced to recognize the independence of Finland and the Baltic states; but in the south it sent troops to set up **soviet** governments in Azerbaijan, Armenia and Georgia. The last major threat came from the Poles, who had invaded the Ukraine in April 1920. The Red Army counter-attacked, but when it tried to follow up its early successes by invading Poland itself it was defeated, and at the Treaty of Riga in 1921 Russia agreed to recognize Polish independence.

Why the Reds won

Why did the Bolsheviks win? Part of the answer lay in the fighting skills of the Red Army,

Russia during the civil war 1918-20.

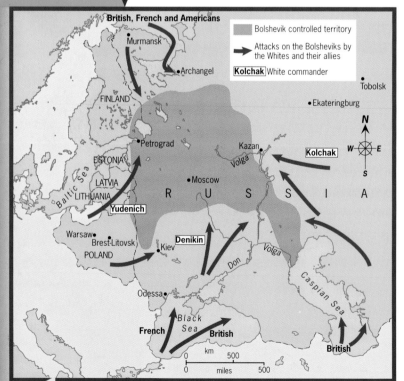

British, French and Americans

- Murmansk
- Archangel

Bolshevik controlled territory

Attacks on the Bolsheviks by the Whites and their allies

Kolchak White commander

FINLAND

- Tobolsk
- Ekateringburg

- Petrograd

ESTONIA

LATVIA

LITHUANIA

Yudenich

Baltic Sea

- Warsaw
- Brest-Litovsk
- Kiev

POLAND

R U S S I A

- Moscow
- Kazan

Volga

Kolchak

N
W E
S

Volga

Don

Denikin

- Odessa

Black Sea

French

British

km 500
miles 500

Caspian Sea

British

built up from scratch by Trotsky from early 1918 on. At its heart were the **Red Guards**, men recruited from the factories, alongside pro-Bolshevik soldiers and sailors from the old **tsarist** army. It was expanded at first with volunteers, although later conscripts were forced to sign up, with **communists** and workers among the first to be drafted. Eventually all men from the ages of 18 to 40 were called up, creating a force of almost five million men. Although only one in ten of these were front-line troops, many more were involved in administration. For battlefield commanders, Trotsky turned to ex-tsarist officers, sending Bolshevik **commissars** to keep an eye on them and using their families as hostages to ensure their loyalty.

Leon Trotsky, the Bolsheviks' military chief in the civil war, inspects Red Army troops.

Trotsky himself turned out to be an energetic military leader, and he had the advantage of defending a central homeland against enemies who were scattered and out of touch with one another. Yet probably the main reason why the Bolsheviks won was the attitude of the Whites themselves. To win the war, they needed support within Russia — and especially from the peasants, who still made up the vast bulk of the population. They alone could have provided the invading armies with the food they needed to live on and fighting men for their ranks. But the peasants never rallied to the White cause. Although they had no love for the Bolsheviks, the revolution had given them land from the old landowners' estates. They feared that the Whites would take these gains away and give the land back to its old owners — the last thing they wanted to happen.

Their suspicions were only confirmed by the behaviour of the armies, which plundered and killed mercilessly in search of supplies. This spread a 'White terror' that was as bad as the the Red Terror, though on a smaller scale. By failing to win over the peasants, the Whites failed to win over Russia — and they paid the price in defeat and exile.

The last of Lenin

By late 1920 three years of war and revolution had exhausted Russia. Large parts of the countryside had become virtually self-governing. The peasants in many areas had stopped sending food to the towns because they had no wish to earn money that, because of **inflation**, was literally no longer worth the paper it was printed on. The transport system had almost ground to a halt, and within the cities many factories had closed down for lack of raw materials to work with. By 1920 industrial production was just one-seventh of its pre-1914 level. Those who could fled to the countryside in search of food; the population of Petrograd dropped from over two million to just half a million.

War Communism

Driven by the need to support the war, the **Bolsheviks** forced through hardline economic policies. Under so-called 'War Communism', almost all private trade was banned, all industry was brought under state control, and armed bands of **Red Guards** were sent out into the countryside to collect grain by force. In response, some peasants themselves took up arms, with 344 peasant uprisings reported by 1919. Some of the **guerrilla** bands — known as Greens, to distinguish them from the **Whites** and Reds — ended up controlling entire provinces.

The starving children pictured here were victims of the 1921–22 famine. An estimated five million people died of starvation.

With the war's end in 1920, things might have got better, but in fact two years of drought spread famine through the land. In some areas the peasants were driven to cannibalism to fight off starvation. In 1921–22, some five million people died of hunger and disease — more than in World War One and the civil war combined. Even formerly loyal supporters of the government now took up the cause of revolt. There was a **mutiny** at the Kronstadt naval base, long a hotbed of Bolshevism, that was brutally put down with the loss of over 10,000 lives.

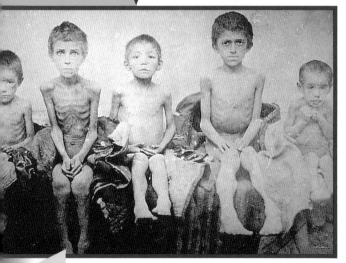

The New Economic Policy

In 1921, faced with economic ruin and a rising tide of protest, Lenin decided on a change of direction. In place of the harsh, state-run approach of War Communism, he brought in the 'New Economic Policy', which once more allowed small-scale trading and returned small factories to private ownership. In place of grain requisitioning, the peasants were to be allowed to sell for profit nine-tenths of the food they grew and the state took only the final tenth as a tax in kind. Old-style management and accounting practices were reintroduced, and productive workers were paid higher wages than unproductive ones.

Some **left-wing** Bolsheviks saw the New Economic Policy as a betrayal of their ideals, but the results were dramatic as agricultural and industrial output both improved rapidly. Meanwhile, the revolution forged ahead in the fields of education and women's rights. Free schooling for all children was introduced, and as a result literacy rates (the proportion of the population that can read and write) climbed spectacularly. Women received equal treatment with men before the law with divorce and abortion available on demand. Only in the political field was there no loosening of the

The body of Lenin lies in state after his death in January 1924. Half a million people queued in freezing temperatures to view the corpse.

Stepping back to leap further

In a 1921 speech, Lenin explained why he introduced the New Economic Policy: 'We are now retreating, going back as it were, but we are doing this to retreat first and then run forward more vigorously. We retreated on this one condition alone when we introduced our New Economic Policy — so as to begin a more determined offensive after the retreat.'

reins. In 1921 opposition groups were banned even within the Bolshevik Party itself which from that year on became known as the **Communist Party**. Hostility to the Church also worsened. In February 1922, a decree was issued stating that all church valuables should be seized by the state, and several thousand priests were killed in the persecution that followed.

In May 1922, soon after introducing the new programme, Lenin had a stroke, setting off a struggle for power within the Party over who should succeed him. When he finally died, in January 1924, he was given a hero's farewell. Half a million people queued to pay their last respects. His body was enshrined in a specially-built mausoleum (grand tomb) in Moscow's Red Square. Weirdly, his brain was removed and cut into 30,000 slices, supposedly to permit future scientists to study the nature of his genius; the segments are preserved in Moscow to this day. To honour Lenin, Petrograd, the former St Petersberg, was renamed Leningrad.

Russia and the outside world

Lenin and his fellow **Bolsheviks** had always believed that the Russian revolution would be the trigger for other **communist** uprisings around the globe. They believed that their success would mark a **socialist** dawn that would launch a new age in world history.

By the time of Lenin's death, though, it was becoming clear that the rest of the world was not about to follow the Russian example. In 1922 the regions, such as Georgia, Azerbaijan, Armenia and the Ukraine, that had failed to establish their independence from Moscow after the revolution were formally grouped together in the Union of **Soviet** Socialist Republics (USSR). As for the rest of the world, Lenin's eventual successor Stalin (himself a Georgian) came to the conclusion that for the time being the nation should stop trying to export **communism** and should instead concentrate on building up Russia's economic and military strength — a policy known as 'building socialism in one country'.

Stalin seizes power

Stalin had not been Lenin's choice as his successor — in a secret memo, he had called him too coarse and intolerant — and Stalin soon lived up to Lenin's worst fears. Through clever political manoeuvring he managed to gain total control of the **Communist Party** and then set about eliminating all his rivals. Trotsky was driven into **exile** in 1929 and was **assassinated** in Mexico on Stalin's orders eleven years later. By that time most of the old Bolshevik leadership had been killed following a series of **show trials** in which the accused were forced to confess to unlikely charges of treason or conspiracy and then executed.

With all opposition cowed into silence by his reign of terror, Stalin ruled as a **dictator**, using his powers to push through **radical** changes in Russian society. He succeeded in **industrializing** the USSR through a series of five-year plans. In the countryside he did away with the old village communes and forced the peasants to work as employees on **collective farms** run on factory lines; millions died in futile attempts to resist this policy.

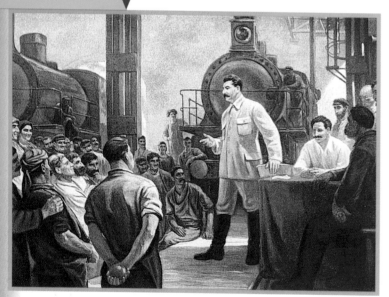

This painting shows Stalin in 1926 giving a speech to workers at a railway engine factory. Stalin was determined to industrialize the USSR. His tough policies led to a dramatic increase in industrial production in the years before World War Two.

Stalin lived in constant fear of attack, not just from enemies within Russia but also from foreign powers. In the 1930s, he had good reason to fear the intentions of **Nazi** Germany. Its leader, Adolf Hitler, was committed to destroying Soviet communism. After making a temporary alliance of convenience with his arch-enemy in the Nazi-Soviet Pact of 1939, designed to buy time to build up the Red Army, Stalin had to cope with a full-scale German invasion from 1941 on.

The Soviet Union during the Cold War years.

The coming of the Cold War

For four years, during World War Two, the USSR fought for its life, helped by the USA and Britain, its partners in the war against Nazism. Victory in 1945, however, soon gave way to the development of tensions between these three powers. Stalin's successful attempts to force communist rule on the countries adjoining the USSR's western borders, in particular Poland, Czechoslovakia and Hungary, raised fears that the nation had moved from 'socialism in one country' to nothing less than a drive for world domination. The result was the **Cold War**, which for the next 45 years effectively split much of the world into hostile communist and anti-communist camps. To its enemies, the new Russian empire, was more dictatorial and repressive than anything known in the time of the **tsars**.

In March 1946 Britain's war leader Winston Churchill spoke of the new division of Europe. 'A shadow has fallen across the scenes so lately lighted by the Allied victory. From Stettin on the Baltic to Trieste on the Adriatic an iron curtain has descended across the continent...' Nowhere was this more evident than in the divided German city of Berlin where the USSR built a wall to stop East Berliners escaping to the West.

The Soviet collapse

US President Kennedy (right) and Soviet Premier Khrushchev (left) pictured here in Vienna in 1961. A year later their two countries almost went to war when the US discovered Russian nuclear missiles on the neighbouring island of Cuba.

The **Cold War** world that emerged out of World War Two was one of fear on both sides. The **Western allies** feared the spread of **communism** around the world. Stalin feared their policy of containment, which looked to him like an attempt to throttle Russia, much as, in his view, the Allies had tried to stamp out **Bolshevism** by their interventions in the civil war. The alarm on each side was increased by the knowledge that the other had nuclear weapons that could destroy entire nations, if not the world itself.

For over 40 years the Cold War blew hot and cold as global crises came and went. There was a temporary improvement in relations after the death of Stalin in 1953. The subsequent Russian campaign of 'destalinization', aimed at exposing some of the excesses of his rule. The climate chilled again in 1956, when the Russians sent troops to bloodily suppress a popular uprising against **Soviet** rule in Hungary. The Cold War reached an all-time low in 1962, when US President John F. Kennedy received evidence that Russian missiles were being sent to Cuba, a **communist**-run island situated just 250 kilometres (156 miles) off the American coast. For a few days the threat of nuclear war loomed. At the last moment the Russian Premier Nikita Khruschev agreed to withdraw the weapons and the world breathed a collective sigh of relief.

Costs of the Cold War

Meanwhile, the pressure of non-stop military rivalry with the USA was having a damaging effect on the USSR. The Bolsheviks had believed that a communist system in which people worked for the benefit of society as a whole would quickly outstrip a **capitalist** one based on individual greed. In practice, though, it was the capitalist USA that provided the best standard of living for its workers and delivered the fastest economic growth. It also proved better at delivering the goods that people wanted. The strain of heavy and continued spending on arms held back the much smaller Russian economy. Meanwhile, the high hopes of an equal society that had buoyed up the Bolsheviks had slowly drained away. Ordinary Russians saw that **Communist Party bureaucrats** enjoyed a high standard of living while they still had difficulty getting the basic necessities.

The final straw came in Afghanistan, where the Red Army intervened in 1979 to force a pro-Russian ruler on a passionately Muslim people. The war lasted nine years, draining the USSR's human and material resources. At the same time, under President Ronald Reagan, the USA was embarking on a fresh round of military spending on an expensive new strategic defence programme, dubbed 'Star Wars' by the media. The USSR simply could not keep up.

Changing the system

When a new, dynamic leader, Mikhail Gorbachev, came to power in Moscow in 1985, he saw the need for change. Preaching the doctrine of *glasnost* (openness) and *perestroika* (economic restructuring), he turned his back on almost 70 years of centralized planning by the state. At the same time he abandoned the arms race with the West, driving forward a large-scale programme of weapons cuts. Among the first to benefit from the new climate of freedom were the USSR's unwilling partners in eastern Europe, which took the opportunity to declare their independence from Soviet control. The new era was symbolized by the breaking down, in 1989, of the Berlin Wall. East and West Germany were reunited. Poland, Hungary, Czechoslovakia, Lithuania, Romania and Bulgaria all elected their own governments in the early years of the 1990s.

While East German border guards look on passively, a West German demonstrator takes a sledgehammer to the Berlin Wall. The demolition of the wall in 1989 symbolically marked the end of the Soviet era in eastern Europe.

When Boris Yeltsin was voted president in 1991 in the course of Russia's first entirely free elections, Russia finally turned its back on the communist past. Symbolic of this break with the past, Leningrad was renamed St Petersburg. Suddenly the events of 1917 appeared in a new light. They had **radically** changed Russia — indeed the course of world history. They had not, however, set its course for ever, as the Bolsheviks had thought they would.

The legacy of the Russian Revolution

The people who made the Russian Revolution hoped that it would prove to be a model for all humankind. The **Bolsheviks** dreamed of ushering in an age of social justice and universal harmony around the globe. That hope quickly proved unfounded. Under Stalin, Russia experienced terrible injustices and brutal **dictatorship**. In the **Cold War** years the world became more deeply divided, and on one occasion came close to a nuclear war.

The gulags

Those dreaming of a freer and more open country were also disappointed. Criticism of the **communist** system in the USSR was not allowed and opponents of the regime were sent off to forced-labour camps administered by a sinister organization called the gulag. It has been estimated that up to six million **political prisoners** were held in captivity at any one time. During Stalin's dictatorship many in the gulags died from overwork and starvation. After Stalin's death some were released and conditions in these prison camps did improve.

With the abandonment of **communism** in Russia in the 1990s, it became easy to see the revolution as no more than a terrible mistake. Yet the events of 1917 had left a positive mark on Russia. The society that emerged from the chaos of the revolution was a much more equal one than anything that had been known under the **tsars**. The Russian people were also better educated. Compulsory schooling had lessened the hold of superstition on the minds of the people of this vast country.

Russia's progress from communism to democracy has not been easy. During the late 1990s people were forced to queue for basic products and rising prices caused particular hardship amongst elderly people.

Improvements for women

The status of women had improved. In tsarist times women were expected to do back-breaking work in the fields but had few rights. Under the **Soviet** regime they received equality before the law and were able to do work that had previously been reserved for men. This proved a heavy burden as they were still expected to carry out all their traditional tasks as well.

Economically, Russia had been transformed from a largely agricultural land to one with a huge, though by the 1990s an ageing, industrial base. It also showed it was capable of cutting-edge technological advancement in certain selected fields, notably space research. Some of these changes were starting even under the last tsar, but the revolution speeded them up.

The global impact

The Russian experiment changed the outside world too. Revolutionaries in other countries took inspiration from Lenin's success. One revolutionary leader, Mao Zedong (Tse-tung) turned China into a communist nation in 1949. In the **West** too, many idealistic individuals fell under the spell of communism in the early years, although support for the Russian variety of communism fell away fast from the 1950s onwards after the facts of Stalin's tyranny and of Soviet oppression in eastern Europe became widely known. In the Western **democracies**, fear of a communist take-over was an often unspoken influence leading governments to insist on fairer treatment for their own workers. It is perhaps no coincidence that since the collapse of the USSR the gap between rich and poor has begun to increase once more around the world.

Although the Cold War divided some nations it brought others closer together. Fear of a spread of communism helped create support for the Western alliances like NATO (North Atlantic Treaty Organization formed in 1949). With a communist enemy on their doorstep, Western European economies drew closer together, forming the EEC (European Economic Community, now known as the EU – European Union) during the Cold War Era.

Sadly the high ideals that inspired the Russian Revolution were let down by the undemocratic means used to bring them about. Russia in 1917 proved too deeply divided for change to come about through common consent. Instead it came through confrontation and bloodshed. The results are still being felt around the world to this day.

With the collapse of communism in the Soviet Union, China was left as the world's biggest communist power, with well over one billion people.

Timeline

1861	Tsar Alexander II frees the serfs
1881	Alexander II assassinated by terrorists; he was succeeded by Alexander III
1894	Nicholas II becomes tsar
1898	Social Democratic Party founded
1902	Social Revolutionary Party founded
1903	Trans-Siberian railway completed
	Social Democrats split between Bolsheviks and Mensheviks
1904	Russo-Japanese War breaks out
	V. K. Plehve, minister of the interior, assassinated
1905	'Bloody Sunday' massacre of demonstrators in St Petersburg
	Russia defeated by Japanese in battles of Mukden and Tsushima
	Tsar issues 'October Manifesto', promising constitutional change
1906	'Fundamental Laws' reaffirm autocracy (one-man rule)
	First Duma (parliament) called, to be dissolved after two months
	Peter Stolypin becomes prime minister
1907	New, less democratic, Duma elected
1911	Stolypin assassinated
1914	Outbreak of World War One
	Russia, allied with Britain and France, declares war on Germany and Austria-Hungary
	Russia defeated at Tannenberg and the Masurian Lakes
1915	Tsar Nicholas takes charge of army as commander-in-chief
1916	Rasputin murdered by aristocratic conspirators
1917	March: First revolution forces tsar to abdicate (give up power)
	Provisional Government set up to organize democratic elections
	Russian army suffers fresh defeats in Austria-Hungary
	In the 'July days' riots, Bolsheviks try unsuccessfully to seize power
	Alexander Kerensky takes over as prime minister
	September: General Lev Kornilov stages an unsuccessful military coup
	November: Bolsheviks take over Petrograd (St Petersburg) and proclaim Russian Revolution
1918	January: Bolsheviks dissolve the Constituent Assembly
	Russia makes peace with Germany at Treaty of Brest-Litovsk
	July: Nicholas II and his family murdered
	Civil war breaks out between Red and White forces
1920	Red forces victorious in the civil war
1921	Lenin announces 'New Economic Policy', allowing some private trade
	Famine spreads across Russia
1924	Death of Lenin starts power struggle in Bolshevik Party
1927	Stalin emerges as Russia's unchallenged leader
1939	Nazi-Soviet Pact signed by Germany and Russia

1941	German armies invade Russia
1945	Russia emerges victorious from World War Two but with an estimated 26 million citizens dead
	Start of Cold War
1953	Death of Stalin
1961	Berlin Wall divides East from West Berlin
1962	Cuban missile crisis
1985	Mikhail Gorbachev becomes leader of USSR and announces new policy of glasnost (openness)
1989	Berlin Wall demolished signalling end of Cold War
1991	Boris Yeltsin becomes president of a non-communist Russia
	USSR broken up, to be replaced by Commonwealth of Independent States

Further reading

Reference books

Lenin and the Russian Revolution, Steve Philips, Heinemann Educational, 2000

Lenin's Russia, Alan White, Collins Educational, 1998

The Russian Revolution, Stewart Ross, Wayland, 1988

The Russian Revolution, Adrian Gilbert, Wayland, 1995

The Russian Revolution, Susan Willoughby, Heinemann Library, 1995

First-person accounts

Ten Days that Shook the World, John Reed, Penguin Books, 1977

Witnesses of the Russian Revolution, Harvey Pitcher, Pimlico, 2001

Novels

Dr Zhivago, Boris Pasternak, Harvill Press, 1996

The White Guard, Michael Bulgakov, Harvill Press, 1996

Glossary

allies, Allies friendly countries who agree to support one another. The Allies were a group of countries that fought together in World War One and Two and were on the side of the UK, France and the USA.

aristocracy people who have a high position in society, which they have usually inherited from their parents

assassination murder for political ends

Austria-Hungary Central European empire, broken up after World War One

autocracy one-man rule

Bolshevik faction of Social Democrats following Lenin

bureaucrat privileged office-holder

Cadet member of the Constitutional Democratic party, supporting parliamentary rule

capitalist describing an economic system where factories and businesses are owned by private individuals for their own profit and where government control over those businesses and industries is minimal

censorship banning of information for political or other reasons

Cheka Bolshevik secret police

Cold War 45-year hostilities between capitalist countries (led by USA) and the communist bloc (led by the USSR) after World War Two

collective farm farm in which land, tools, etc are owned in common rather than by individual families

commissar Communist Party official

communism political system where private ownership has been abolished and where factories and industries are run by the state for the benefit of all

communist member of the Communist Party or a word to describe the political system of communism

Communist Party name used by the Bolshevik Party from the 1920s on

Constituent Assembly assembly elected in 1918 that was to work out a new constitution. It was never able to do this as it was broken up by the Bolsheviks.

Cossacks peasant warrior people from the southern Ukraine

counter-revolutionaries people opposed to the forces of revolution

coup armed take-over of power

Crimea peninsula in south Russia extending into the Black Sea

democracy method of governing a country where the people choose their leaders in elections

deputies elected representatives

dictator person who has complete control of a country

diplomacy solving problems through discussions with other nations

Duma name of the parliament called by the tsar after 1905

emancipation to set free, usually from some sort of slavery or bondage

exile being sent away from one's own country or region and not being allowed to return

guerrilla fighter not forming part of a regular army

human rights right of everyone to live without injustice, persecution or discrimination

industrialization policy of encouraging the development of heavy industry

infantry soldiers on foot

inflation widespread rise in prices

left-wing in political terms, leaning towards a socialist or communist viewpoint

Marxist follower of the communist philosophy of the German philosopher Karl Marx

Menshevik faction of Social Democrats opposed to Lenin

militias military forces often made up of civilians

mobilization calling up of an army for war

mutiny revolt against someone in charge, usually in the army or navy

nationalize to bring under state control

Nazi member of the right-wing National Socialist Party in Germany during Hitler's time

patriotism strong feelings of loyalty for one's country

political prisoners people who are imprisoned because of their political beliefs

propaganda information spread for political purposes

Provisional Government temporary government set up to call parliamentary elections after the fall of the tsar in 1917

radicals, radical people who want to make great changes. A radical change is a great change.

Red Guards Bolshevik military force of armed workers

right-wing in political terms, leaning towards a more conservative or monarchist viewpoint

serf peasant tied for life to the service of one landowner

show trial trial held for propaganda purposes

socialism, socialist political system where wealth is shared equally and some of the main industries are run by the government. A socialist is someone who supports this system.

Social Democrats Russian political movement inspired by the views of the political philosopher Karl Marx

Social Revolutionary member of a Russian revolutionary movement that focused on the peasants

soviet, Soviet workers' or peasants' council. This word also became part of the name of the country the Union of Soviet Socialist Republics (USSR).

strike when people refuse to work as a way of making a protest

trade unions organized groups of workers usually set up to help improve both pay and working conditions

tsar desribes Russia's ruler before the Revolution

West, Western political, rather than a geographical name for the industrialized countries of western Europe, North America, Australia and New Zealand

Whites opponents of the Reds (Bolsheviks) in the civil war

working class people who work for wages, often doing manual or industrial work

Index